# The Fairy Tale Life of Hans Christian Andersen

by Eva Moore
Illustrated by Trina Schart Hyman
Cover by Burt Dodson

D0029174

## SCHOLASTIC INC.

New York   Toronto   London   Auckland   Sydney

*For Daddy*

ISBN 0-590-45225-8

12 11 10 9 8 7 6 5 4 3 2 1          4          2 3 4 5 6 7/9

Printed in the U.S.A.                                          40

## A Play

ONCE UPON A TIME — over one hundred
years ago — there lived a little boy named
Hans Christian Andersen. He was the
son of a shoemaker, and he lived in the
country of Denmark, in a little town
called Odense.

Hans's mother and father were very
poor, but they did everything they
could to make him happy.

Hans's father did not have money to
buy toys for his son, so he made the
toys himself. The best toy of all was a
puppet theater and puppets. Five-year-
old Hans never grew tired of watching
the puppets.

"When you are bigger," Hans's father told him many times, "you can make up your own plays."

Every day Hans asked his father to put on a puppet play for him. One day his father said, "Hans Christian, I have a better idea. How would you like to come with me to the playhouse? We will see a real play in a real theater!"

Hans had never seen a real play. "Is it like our plays with the puppets?" he asked his father.

"Better! Much better!" said the shoemaker. He sat down at his workbench. "You will see. Now let your mother dress you. You must wear your best clothes to the theater."

Hans ran across the room to his mother. She was sitting on the big bed, sewing. The room was so small that Hans could run from his father's workbench to the big bed in a few steps.

This small room was a whole house

for Hans Christian Andersen and his mother and father. The room was cheerful. Pots and jars filled with flowers sat on the windowsill. Pictures were hanging on every wall. Even the back of the door was covered with bright paintings.

The workbench, the big bed, and a small chest of drawers were all the furniture in the small house. Hans's own little bed was pulled out from a closet at night. In the morning the bed was pushed back into the closet so that the family would have room to walk around.

To little Hans everything in the house was wonderful — and the most wonderful thing was the ladder. The ladder was built against a wall. It went up the wall and out to the roof. On the roof was a tiny garden where Hans's mother grew vegetables. Sometimes Hans would climb up the ladder and play on the roof. How far down the street looked! Hans felt he was on top of the world.

But now Hans had no time to play on the roof. He had something more important to do. He was going to the theater.

Hans's mother dressed Hans in his best suit of clothes.

"Your shirt is so plain," she said to him. "If only you had a bright waistcoat to wear over it."

Where could she get one for Hans? There, over on the workbench, she saw pieces of silk cloth — red, blue, and green. Hans's father was going to make clothes for the puppets out of the silk.

"I can use that cloth to make a pretty waistcoat for Hans Christian," Mrs. Andersen said, and the shoemaker gave her the pieces of silk.

There was no time for Hans's mother to sew them together, so she pinned them onto Hans's shirt — a red one here, a blue one there, a green one, and another blue one.

"Oh, look at Hans!" she cried to her husband. "Doesn't he look pretty? All he needs now is a tie to wear."

Hans had no tie. But on the chest of drawers was a yellow handkerchief.

"Aha!" cried Mrs. Andersen. She grabbed the handkerchief and put it around Hans's neck. She tied it into a big bow under his chin. Then she combed Hans's straight blond hair and put on his wooden shoes. Hans was ready to go.

Clumpety-clump, clump. Hans's heavy wooden shoes banged against the stone streets as he walked at his father's side.

People turned to stare at the little boy in the red and blue and green waistcoat and the big yellow bow.

When Hans and his father came near the Odense Playhouse, Hans's father said, "Look, Hans Christian, there it is. There is the theater!"

Hans tugged on his father's hand and pulled him to the door. Inside the theater, Hans saw rows and rows of chairs. And in every chair someone was sitting. Rows and rows of people! Hans had never seen so many people together in one place.

"Oh, Father!" he said. "If only we had as many tubs of butter as there are people here — then I would eat lots of butter!"

"Hans Christian," his father said, "if you ate that much butter, you would get sick." The shoemaker gently brushed Hans's hair off his forehead.

"Yet you get little enough of any food to eat," he thought sadly as he looked at Hans's thin legs and arms. "And it is my fault. If I made more money, you would eat well. Yes, we might even have as many tubs of butter as there are people here. But I am too poor, and I will always be too poor."

Just then, the people in the theater stopped talking and everyone looked at the stage. The curtain went up, and Hans Christian Andersen saw a real play for the first time in his life.

## The Comet

ONE MORNING Hans was up on the roof, helping his mother weed the garden. It was so quiet that Hans could hear a small pop whenever he pulled out a weed. Then he heard a loud shout from the street below.

"Look! Look in the sky!" someone yelled.

Hans and his mother looked up. Even though it was day, they saw a star. But it was not like any star they had seen before. It was big and round and there was a tail of light streaming out from it.

"What does it mean?" Hans's mother cried.

Now people were coming out of the houses. They stood in the street below, looking at the star.

"It is surely a bad sign," one of them said. "It means something terrible is going to happen. It might even mean that the world is coming to an end."

"The end of the world!" Hans's mother said, and she held her little boy tightly in her arms.

All the people started to talk at once. Some began to cry.

Then Hans's father came running out of the house. "What is it?" he said. "What is the matter?"

"Look!" someone said and pointed to the thing in the sky.

"Why — it's a comet!" Hans's father cried. "How lucky we are to see it."

"How can you say that?" Hans's mother called down from the roof. "It means the end of the world."

"No, no," the shoemaker said. "A comet is only a ball of fire — like a star. It is in the sky, thousands and thousands of miles away. It is not a sign of anything — it is only what it is. There is nothing to be afraid of."

Hans could tell that his mother and the other people did not believe his father. And Hans was afraid too.

All day the comet burned in the sky, but the world did not come to an end.

That night Hans's little bed was pulled out of the closet as it was every night, and his mother tucked him in. But it was a long time before Hans went to sleep. Even when he closed his eyes, he seemed to see the comet shining brightly in the sky.

## School

A FEW DAYS after the comet disappeared, Hans was playing out in the yard. He had one of his mother's big aprons and two long sticks. Hans put the sticks into the ground near the currant bush he had planted himself. He hung the apron over the sticks and the bush. Now he had a tent. He went inside.

Everything was shadowy and quiet under the apron-tent. Hans looked at the shadows the leaves of the currant bush made on the apron. He pretended each shadow was a tiny elf. He talked and sang to the shadow elves. Then he heard his mother calling him.

"Come inside, Hans Christian," Mrs. Andersen called. "You must change into your good clothes."

"Maybe I am going to the theater again!" thought Hans. He crawled out of his tent.

"Where am I going, Mother?" Hans asked when he came to the house. "Am I going to see another play?"

"No," Mrs. Andersen said. "You are going to school to learn to read and write. I am taking you to the ABC school."

Hans did not want to go. He had heard the older children talk about the ABC school.

"But Mother," he said, "the teacher is mean. She carries a stick to beat children. She will beat me."

"If that teacher ever hits you with a stick," said Hans's mother, "get up and run home. I will not send you back. I promise."

Mrs. Andersen washed Hans's hair and curled it. She dressed him in his best suit. When his hair was dry, she combed it out. Hans looked in the mirror. He saw big curls all over his head. That afternoon Hans walked to the school-house with his mother.

Now Hans was a schoolboy. Every day he had to go to school. The school was one big room. The children sat on long benches. The teacher stood in front of them with her big stick in her hand. When she said to the class, "Spell cat," all the children had to spell it out loud together — "C-A-T."

When the teacher asked the children, "How much is two and two?" they all had to say the answer out loud together. If the teacher saw that someone was not saying the lesson, she hit him with her stick. All the children were afraid of that stick.

Hans didn't like school. He did not like to sit on the hard bench and say the lessons out loud. He wanted to go home and sit under his apron-tent.

There was only one thing in the school Hans liked — the clock. Every hour, a little door in the clock would open and some little dolls would come out.

One day Hans was watching the clock, waiting to see the dolls come out. He forgot all about the lesson. The teacher saw that he was not spelling out loud with the rest of the class.

SMACK! She hit Hans with her stick.

Hans did not say a word. He jumped up and grabbed his book. He ran out of the school, and he did not stop until he was home.

"Hans, why are you home so early?" his mother asked him. "Is school over already?"

Hans began to cry. "The teacher hit me — she hit me with her stick," he said. "I don't ever want to go back to that school again."

Hans's mother put her arms around him. "I will keep my promise," she said. "You will not have to go back to the ABC school. You can stay at home with me."

Hans's father looked up from his workbench. "But Hans must learn how to read and write. We will find another school for him."

And they did. Soon Hans was going to Mr. Carsten's school for poor boys. Most of the other boys were older than Hans. He was only six years old and he was the smallest boy in the class.

Mr. Carsten was kind and did not carry a stick. Hans liked him, but he did not learn much in school. He never paid attention to the lessons. He could hardly wait until school was out. Then he would run home to his father and the wonderful puppet theater.

## The Dancing Shoes

"First you do a dance, like this. Then you make a bow, like that!" Hans Christian Andersen said to his puppet. Hans made the puppet dance and bow. "And now" — Hans picked up another puppet — "we will have a play." Hans made the play up as he went along.

Hans was almost eight years old now — old enough to make up plays and sew clothes for the puppets. Often Hans and his father put on a puppet show together. But today Mr. Andersen was too busy to play with Hans. He was making a special pair of shoes. They were dancing shoes for a rich lady who lived in the country, a few miles away.

The rich lady wanted a shoemaker to make all the shoes for her family. She would give this shoemaker a pretty house to live in. There would be a garden in front of the house and a field in back. There would be room for a cow in the field.

Hans's father was happy when he heard about the job. How wonderful it would be to have a big house in the country, he thought, with a real garden. And they could buy a cow! The cow would give milk. And from the milk, they could make butter — lots of butter for Hans Christian to eat!

Hans's father had gone to see the rich lady to ask for the job. She had given him some pink silk cloth.

"Use this to make a pair of dancing shoes for me," she had said. "If I like the shoes, you will have the job."

The shoemaker bought the best leather he could get to make soles for the dancing shoes. He cut out the soles very slowly. But he cut them crooked.

Hans's father bought more leather. He cut out another pair of soles. Then he cut the pink silk for the top part of the dancing shoes. The pieces of silk came out a little crooked too, but there was no cloth left to make another pair.

Hans's father sewed the silk and the soles together with great care. At last the shoes were finished.

Hans and his mother looked at the dancing shoes. "You have never made a better pair of shoes," Mrs. Andersen said. "They are fit for a princess."

"I will take them to the lady now," said Hans's father. He took off his apron and put on his cap. He wrapped the pink silk dancing shoes in a handkerchief and was on his way.

Hans stood at the door with his mother. They watched as the shoemaker walked away. His head was high, and he was humming a tune.

"Just think, Hans Christian," said Mrs. Andersen. "We will have a new house. We will have a garden and a cow!"

All day Hans and his mother talked about the country and what they would do when they lived there. The more they talked, the happier they felt. They laughed and hugged each other.

Hours passed, but Hans's father did not come back. Hans and his mother kept jumping up and going outside to look for him.

More hours passed. The sun went down. The sky was almost dark. Then, at last, they saw him coming.

But what was wrong? He was walking slowly with his head down. Was he looking for something he had dropped on the ground?

Hans and his mother ran to meet the shoemaker. When he heard them coming, he looked up. There were tears in his eyes.

"I gave the dancing shoes to the lady," he said. He was so angry he could hardly speak. "She took one look at them and threw them back to me. She said they were no good. She said I had spoiled her silk. I did not get the job."

After that, Hans's father was never happy when he was working at his bench. The only time he smiled was when he and Hans were playing with the puppets, or when he was reading one of his books.

The books were kept in the cupboard over the workbench. They were the only treasures Hans's father had. He went to the cupboard for a book almost every day. Sometimes he read to himself. Many times he read stories from the books to Hans.

Hans liked to hear his father read. And he liked to listen to the stories his mother told him too. She had never learned how to read, but she knew many tales — tales filled with magic and strange people.

While Hans's mother told him stories, his father read the newspaper. There was a war going on. Napoleon, the Emperor of France, was at war with Russia. Many countries were on Russia's side, but Denmark was fighting for Napoleon.

Napoleon was the shoemaker's hero. Now he read in the newspaper that the war was going badly for Napoleon. Mr. Andersen decided to join the army.

Hans was in bed with the measles on the day his father went to war. He lay in the big bed, listening to the drums as the soldiers marched out of Odense. He had never felt so sad. What would happen to his father? Would he ever see him again?

Hans's father did not fight in any battles. But he marched many miles. He slept outside in cold and wet weather. He became weak and thin. When he came home after the war ended, he was a sick man. And he was heartbroken because his hero, Napoleon, had lost.

For a while, Mr. Andersen was able to work at his bench and to play with Hans almost as he used to. But as time went on, Hans saw his father getting thinner and thinner, weaker and weaker.

Then, when Hans was eleven years old, the poor shoemaker died. Hans and his mother were alone.

## The Chinese Prince

"What are you drawing, Hans?" a pretty girl asked Hans Christian Andersen. They sat together on the bank of the Odense River.

"I am drawing a castle," Hans told her. He showed his picture to the girl. "See, here is the outside. And here are the rooms inside."

"It is beautiful!" the girl said. "Who lives in the castle?"

"It is mine," said Hans. "I will live in it when it is built."

The girl laughed. "Yes, and it will be built when you are Prince of Denmark, I suppose."

"Or maybe when I am King of Denmark," said Hans.

"Hans Christian Andersen!" the girl said. "You are just a poor boy who will be lucky to be a carpenter or a shoemaker one day. How can you think of being a king!"

"Who knows what will happen?" Hans said. "Maybe I shall become a king. I shall never be a carpenter or a shoe-maker, I can tell you that!"

"Oh, Hans," the girl said, "you *are* silly!"

She jumped up and walked away.

Hans was used to being left alone like this. Not many of the children wanted to be his friend. He was not like them. He was so strange.

The other children never walked along the street with their eyes closed

— but Hans did sometimes, when he was thinking hard. The other children never spent hours playing with puppets or writing plays — but Hans did. The other children looked like ordinary children — but Hans did not.

Hans was tall for an eleven-year-old boy. He was thin and he had big feet. His face was ugly, with tiny eyes like two green peas and a long, large nose in between.

After the girl left him, Hans walked along the bank of the river. He climbed out onto a flat rock that hung over the water. From here he could see some women washing clothes in the water. One of these women was his mother. All day long she washed clothes for rich people. That was the only way she could earn a living.

Hans lay down on the rock and looked into the gray water of the Odense River. It sang a song to him. Then Hans, too, began to sing. His voice was high and sweet.

"Are you singing to the fish in the water, Hans?" one of the washerwomen called.

Hans did not answer. He went on singing.

Hans was not singing to the fish. He was singing to the people in the country of China. China was on the other side of the world, right under the Odense River. One of the washerwomen had told Hans so, and he believed her.

"Maybe the Prince of China will hear me singing," Hans thought. "Maybe he will come out of the river and take me back with him to China. I will live in his castle and be rich.

"And when I come back to Odense," Hans dreamed on, "I will bring some gold with me. I will build my castle, just as it looks in my drawings."

Every day Hans sang into the water,

waiting to see the face of the Prince of China come up to him. But the only face he saw in the water was his own. Every day when he left the rock to go home, Hans said to himself, "Tomorrow. Tomorrow might very well be the day I go to China with the Prince."

## The Danish Prince

HANS NEVER WENT to China with the Chinese Prince. He stayed in Odense with his mother.

When Hans was thirteen years old, his mother married again. Now Hans had a stepfather. The family moved into a little house near the river.

Hans's stepfather did the same kind of work his father had done — he was a shoemaker. But he earned even less money, and Hans's mother had to go on washing clothes in the river.

Hans's stepfather did not care if Hans

went to school or not. Hans was free to do whatever he pleased.

Hans liked to stand in the small garden outside his new house and sing. The people who lived nearby would come out to hear him. Sometimes they asked Hans to come into their homes and sing for them. Hans also read poems for them and acted out little plays that he wrote himself.

To Hans there was nothing more wonderful than singing and acting. He made up his mind to become a famous actor.

The grownups liked to have Hans sing and act for them. But no one thought he could ever be an actor on the stage. He was too ugly. He was too clumsy. It would be better if he learned a trade, they thought. Even his mother would not listen when he talked of becoming an actor. She wanted him to be a fine tailor.

"Learn a trade," Hans heard from all the grownups he knew — all but his friend Colonel Guldberg.

"Go to high school and get a good education," Colonel Guldberg told him. "Then you will be able to make a good living all your life." But Colonel Guldberg knew that high school cost a lot of money. He knew that a poor boy like Hans could not go unless someone paid for him.

"I will take you to Odense castle to see Prince Christian," he said to Hans. "Tell the Prince that you want to go to high school. Maybe he will be able to help you."

A few days later, Colonel Guldberg and Hans walked to the Odense castle. They walked across the wide green lawn and up to the big white building. A guard pulled the door open for them, and they went inside.

The Prince of Denmark sat in a big

chair at the end of a long room. Colonel Guldberg introduced Hans to the Prince.

"This is Hans Christian Andersen, Your Highness," he said. "He is the son of a poor washerwoman. He is very smart. And he can sing and act too."

"I would be happy to sing a song for you, Your Highness," Hans said to the Prince.

"I would like to hear it," the Prince answered.

Hans sang a song. Then he acted out part of a play. He recited a poem.

"What an odd boy," the Prince thought as he watched Hans. "He is as funny to watch as a puppet!"

When Hans was done, the Prince sat still for a moment, looking at Hans. Then he cleared his throat.

"Well, Hans Christian Andersen," he said. "You know how to sing and recite, I see. But tell me, what else do you know? How will you make your living?"

"Colonel Guldberg thinks I should go to school and get a good education," Hans answered.

"But what about you?" the Prince asked. "What do *you* want to do?"

Hans looked at Colonel Guldberg. He looked at the Prince. Should he tell Prince Christian that he wanted to go to school? There was only one thing that he really wanted to do.

"I . . . I . . . I want to be an actor in the theater!" he said.

Colonel Guldberg was angry. The Prince of Denmark was angry.

"A boy like you would not have much luck in the theater," the Prince said. "It is hard to become a good actor. Choose a trade instead. Why not be a carpenter?"

Hans did not want to be a carpenter. He wanted to be an actor. And no one — not even the Prince of Denmark — could make him change his mind.

## Good-bye to Odense

WHEN HANS was fourteen years old, he had a chance to act in a real play. A group of actors came to Odense from Copenhagen, the capital city of Denmark. They came from the most famous theater in the country — the Royal Theater. They were going to put on some plays for the people of Odense.

Hans made friends with the actors. They let him watch as they practiced their plays in the Odense Playhouse. Hans told them how much he, too, loved to act. He told them that he wanted to be a famous actor himself. He showed them how he could sing and act.

The actors laughed at Hans — he looked so silly on the stage. But they liked him. And to make him happy, they let him have a small part in one of their plays — the opera *Cinderella*.

Now Hans could not wait any longer to become a real actor. He must go to Copenhagen and get a job in the Royal Theater right away. He had saved some money he earned by running errands. He had thirteen rix-dollars — more than enough to pay his way to Copenhagen. He would use the rest of the money to pay for a room and food until he got a job in the Royal Theater.

Hans told his mother about his plan.

"Why do you want to go away and be an actor?" she said. "You could be a fine tailor here in Odense. Just look at the beautiful clothes you sew for your puppets."

"But I don't want to be a tailor," Hans

told her. "I was meant for something better."

"What will you do in a big city all by yourself?" Hans's mother said, and she began to cry. "How will you get along with no one to love you? What will become of you?"

"I will become famous," Hans answered. "I will earn a lot of money and buy you a beautiful house. Then you will never have to wash clothes in the river again."

But Hans's mother could not stop worrying. What if she let Hans go to the city alone? How could she be sure he would be safe?

Then Mrs. Andersen thought of the old wise woman. People said that the wise woman could look into the future. Maybe she could see what was going to happen to Hans.

Hans's mother took him to see the wise woman. "Tell me what will become of my son," she said.

The old woman put some cards on the table. She looked and looked at the row of cards. At last she lifted her head.

"I have read the cards," she told Mrs. Andersen. "This is what they tell me: Your son will become a great man. The world will love him. One day the town of Odense will pay him a great honor. Everyone will hold a lighted torch to salute him."

Hans's mother believed the wise woman. She was not afraid any more. Hans was free to go to Copenhagen.

On September 4, 1819, Hans got ready to leave Odense. He put on his only suit of clothes — a suit made out of his father's old coat — and his only pair of boots. The boots were brand-new. They were the first pair of leather boots Hans ever had. He liked to hear them squeak as he walked. Hans wanted everyone to see that he had new boots, so he tucked the bottom of his pants into the top of the boots.

Then, Hans put on an old top hat that Colonel Guldberg gave him. The hat was too big for Hans — it kept falling down over his eyes.

Hans's mother put his shirts and underwear and stockings in a small bundle and gave the bundle to Hans. Together they walked to the gates of the town. There was the stagecoach that would take Hans part of the way to Copenhagen.

"Be careful, Hans Christian," his mother said, and she stood on tip-toe to kiss him.

"I will, Mother," Hans promised.
"Don't worry." He climbed into the
stagecoach.

"Giddyap!" the driver called to the
horses. The stagecoach jerked and began
to move.

"Good-bye! Good-bye! Good-bye,
Hans Christian!" called Mrs. Andersen.

"Good-bye!" called Hans, and he
leaned out of the window, holding his
hat on his head with one hand. With the
other hand he waved good-bye to his
mother. He waved until he could not
see her any more.

## Copenhagen

THE TOWN OF ODENSE was on an island.
The stagecoach took Hans to the end of
the island. To get to Copenhagen, he had
to take a ferryboat across the water.
Then he got on another stagecoach. This
stagecoach took him most of the way to
Copenhagen. The trip took two days.

From the high hill where he got off
the stagecoach, Hans could see the roofs
of the buildings in the big city. Some
were bright red. Some were copper.
Hans could see the church steeples
and the masts of fishing boats in
Copenhagen's port. He could see the
long arms of the windmills that stood

near the edge of town.

Hans had a long way to walk to reach the city, and he hurried along. When he passed through the city gate, he saw an inn. "This will be a good place to stay," he thought, and he took a room.

Hans put his bundle of clothes in the room. And then he set out for the main part of town. He had an important letter to deliver.

The letter was for Madame Schall, a famous ballet dancer. Hans had heard the actors of the Royal Theater talk about Madame Schall. She was very important, they said. They talked about her so much that Hans thought she must be the Queen of Everything. He thought someone who was that important would be a good person for him to know.

And so Hans had asked a friend to write a letter about him that he could take to the famous lady. When Madame Schall read the letter, she would want to talk to Hans herself. Then Hans could show her what a good actor and singer he was, and she might help him get a part in a play. This was Hans's plan.

Hans hurried along the narrow streets of Copenhagen. People rushing by almost knocked him over. He saw an old woman selling flowers, and he asked her how to find the street where Madame Schall lived. Soon he was climbing the steps of Madame Schall's house.

But Hans did not ring the bell right away. At the top of the steps, he took off his hat. He got down on his knees to pray. He prayed that Madame Schall would read the letter and help him.

As Hans was praying, a maid came up the steps behind him. She saw him there on his knees, holding his hat upside down in front of him.

"This must be some poor beggar," she thought, and she put some pennies into Hans's hat.

Hans jumped to his feet.

"What are you doing?" he asked the maid.

"I'm giving you some pennies," she said.

"But I am not a beggar," said Hans. "I am an actor. I have come to see Madame Schall. I have a letter that will tell her about me."

"I will take the letter to Madame Schall," the maid said. "Wait here," and she started to go inside with the letter.

"But the pennies . . ." Hans called after her.

"Keep them," the girl said. "I think you may need them more than I." The door shut in Hans's face.

Hans sat down on the top step and waited. He waited and waited.

At last the door opened again, and

the maid brought Hans inside.

When Hans saw Madame Schall, he made a low bow.

"Are you the actor I have read about in this letter?" Madame Schall asked.

"Yes, I am Hans Christian Andersen," Hans said.

Madame Schall had never seen an actor like this before. He looked more like a clown.

"And what parts do you think you can play?" the dancer asked him.

"I know *Cinderella*," Hans answered at once. "Let me show you. I can do all the songs and dances for you."

First Hans took off his boots. "I can dance better without boots," he told the surprised lady.

Then he began to sing, tapping on his hat the way he would tap on a tambourine. He danced around the room in his stocking feet. He tried hard to sing and dance well.

But to Madame Schall, Hans looked
like a tall, thin monkey jumping about
wildly. She had never seen anybody
dance that way. She thought Hans must
be crazy.

"Stop! Stop!" she cried. "I have seen
enough!" She called her maid. "Get rid
of him," she whispered, and she ran out
of the room.

## The Singing Teacher

Hᴀɴs ᴡᴀs ᴏᴜᴛ on the street in front of Madame Schall's house. He could not believe what had happened. What was wrong with Madame Schall? he wondered. Why didn't she let him finish? And now, what would he do?

Hans decided to go straight to the Royal Theater and ask for a job. Maybe he didn't need Madame Schall to help him. Maybe the manager of the theater would give him a job.

But the manager of the Royal Theater would not hire the boy from Odense. "You are too thin to be an actor on the stage," he told Hans.

"But if you hire me and pay me a hundred rix-dollars, I will soon get fat!" Hans said.

The manager would not listen. "We do not need any more actors," he said at last and walked away.

Hans could not find a job, and his money was running out. On his fourth day in Copenhagen, the landlord of the inn asked Hans to pay for his room. Now Hans had less than one rix-dollar left — all he could buy for his breakfast was a loaf of bread.

Hans walked along the docks, and looked at the fishing boats while he ate his bread. "What am I to do now?" he thought. "I cannot go back to Odense until I am famous. But how can I stay here without any money?"

Hans kept on walking and thinking. Suddenly he remembered another famous person in Copenhagen — a man named Siboni. Siboni was the head of a big music school. Hans had read about him in the Odense newspaper.

"Someone like Siboni might want to help a poor boy who can sing as well as I do," Hans thought. He set off to find Siboni's house.

That afternoon, Siboni's housekeeper opened the door and saw Hans Christian Andersen.

"I would like to talk to Mr. Siboni," Hans said.

"He is eating dinner with some friends," the housekeeper told Hans. She was about to shut the door.

"I must see Mr. Siboni," Hans begged. "It is very important." His eyes filled with tears.

The housekeeper let Hans come inside. "What do you want?" she asked.

Hans told her all about himself. He told her about everything that had happened to him since he came from Odense.

"And now I must go back," he said, "unless I can find someone to help me. I love to sing, and my friends tell me I have a good voice. I thought that Mr. Siboni might know of a job for me."

The housekeeper felt sorry for Hans. "I will go to Mr. Siboni and tell him about you," she said.

In a little while, the housekeeper came out of the dining room. And right behind her was Siboni himself, and all his friends.

"So you are the boy who loves to sing," Siboni said. "Sing for us. We would like to hear."

Hans had never been afraid to sing for anyone — not even for the Prince of Denmark. But now he was afraid. He knew he must please Siboni or he would have to go back to Odense, a failure.

Hans closed his eyes and took a deep breath. He pretended he was back in Odense, lying on the rock near the river. And when he sang, he pretended he was singing to a prince in China, deep under the water.

At the end of the song, Hans opened his eyes. Siboni was smiling! All the men clapped.

"Bravo!" said Siboni. "You sing with your heart as well as your voice. You will be a great singer someday."

"Yes!" said Hans. "That is what I would like more than anything in the world."

Siboni and his friends could see that this was true. And they all wanted to help Hans. Siboni would give him free singing lessons until he had learned enough to get a part in an opera. The other men got together and collected money for Hans — seventy rix-dollars! Hans would get ten rix-dollars of this money every month. He would have enough money to stay in Copenhagen for seven months!

Hans was so happy he cried. That night he wrote a letter to his mother. She could not read it herself, but one of her friends read it to her.

*"I have been in the city four days and I have already made many friends,"* Hans had written. *"It will not be long before I am a famous man."*

## The Elves' Sun

SIBONI GAVE HANS free singing lessons for half a year. Then Hans's voice changed. He could no longer sing well. No more singing lessons for Hans.

Then Hans took acting lessons. He tried hard, but his teacher was sure Hans would never be able to act. No more acting lessons for Hans.

Then Hans took ballet lessons. His teacher this time was a dancer named Dahlen. Dahlen liked Hans very much. He could see that Hans loved to dance. He could also see that Hans was too thin and clumsy ever to be a good dancer. But Dahlen went on giving Hans dancing lessons anyway.

April 2, 1822, was Hans Christian Andersen's birthday. He was seventeen years old. Almost three years had gone by since he came to Copenhagen to become a famous actor. Hans was not an actor yet. He was not famous. He did not even have a job.

But Hans did have friends. Many of them were rich. Many of them — like Dahlen — were famous. His friends did whatever they could to help Hans. And when he needed money, they put money in the bank for him. Hans used the money to pay for his room and for food.

Hans's friend Dahlen wrote many ballets for the Royal Theater. He usually picked the best dancers in his dancing class to be in the ballets. But for one ballet he let the worst dancer in the class have a part. Hans Christian Andersen would dance the part of a ghostly spirit. His name would be printed on the

program along with all the other dancers.

The night of the ballet Hans danced with all his heart. And when the ballet was over, he took the program home to his room. The room was not much bigger than a closet. It was as dark as a closet because there were no windows. In this little room, Hans read the program by the light of a candle. He read his name over and over again.

"If only I could dance in ballets all the time! If only I could become famous. Then I might even have enough money to pay back all my friends."

As usual, Hans's biggest worry was money. He had to live on the money his friends put in the bank for him. He used almost all of it to pay for his little room. He never had enough food to eat. He never had enough warm clothes to wear.

Hans tried to forget his troubles. He made a puppet theater and put on puppet shows for Dahlen's children and for the children of his other friends. Sometimes Hans would make cut-outs for the children. As they watched, he folded a plain piece of paper and cut it with his scissors. When he unfolded the paper there would be a beautiful picture. Hans could make so many different pictures that the children thought his scissors must be magic.

Hans told the children stories too — stories he had heard when he was a child, and stories he made up himself. He was a good storyteller. He pretended he was putting on a play when he told a story. He would act it all out. Even though the story was make-believe, he made it seem real.

When Hans was alone in his little room, he liked to read. And he liked to write. He wrote poems. He wrote plays and put them on in his puppet theater.

As the days went by, Hans had less and less money to spend. Soon there would be nothing left in the bank. "My friends won't go on giving me money forever," he thought. "I must earn some myself, somehow."

Hans decided to write a play and sell it to the Royal Theater. He wrote a sad play and called it "The Elves' Sun." He read it to all his friends. One of them sent the play to the directors of the Royal Theater.

The directors of the Royal Theater read this sad play — and they laughed. They laughed at the terrible spelling and bad grammar. It was easy to see that this young writer had never learned how to write or spell correctly. If he had a good education, the directors thought, he might become a good writer.

The directors of the Royal Theater asked Hans to come to see them.

"We have read your play," one man told him. "It is not good enough to be put on in the theater. But we think that someday you may be able to write a play that will be good enough. We think you should have a chance to go to high school and learn to write better.

"And so," he went on, "we are willing to send you to high school. Would you like to go?"

Hans had never wanted to go to high school. He had always been too poor — and besides, he had wanted to be an actor. But now Hans knew that he would never become famous as an actor, or a singer, or a dancer. "Maybe," he thought, "I was born to be a famous writer."

He said to the directors, "Yes, I would like to go to school."

## Master Meisling

Four horses pulling a stagecoach came trotting fast down a dirt road. The stagecoach was going from Copenhagen to the town of Slagelse, twelve miles away. Hans Christian Andersen was riding inside with other schoolboys. They were all going to the same school — the Slagelse Latin School.

Hans was the only one who was going there for the first time. He was the only one who was glad to be going to school.

"Just wait," one of the boys said to Hans. "Just wait until you have been in school for a few weeks. You will be sorry you ever came."

Hans did not think so. He knew he was lucky to be going to high school at all. He was going to work hard and learn all he could. He would write many good plays for the Royal Theater.

Hans wanted the directors of the Royal Theater to be proud of him — especially Jonas Collin. Mr. Collin had promised to look after Hans. He would see that Hans had everything he needed — clothes, books, and a room to sleep in.

In the past few weeks, Hans had been to Mr. Collin's home many times. He was always welcome there. Hans was almost a part of the family now. He loved Mr. Collin's children as if they were his own brother and sisters. Mr. Collin was like a father to him.

Hans would miss the Collins, but he knew he would see them again when he came back to Copenhagen for holidays.

In the meantime, he could write letters to tell them what he was doing in school. And they could write to him.

The stagecoach passed through the gates of a small town and stopped. This was the town of Slagelse. Hans spent his first night at the inn. Then he moved into his own room in a little cottage.

Hans loved his room. It was small but cheerful — and it had a window! Hans could look out and see grass and flowers and sunshine.

"How lucky I am!" he thought. "How happy I am going to be here."

But Hans was not happy for long. His troubles began on the first day of school.

Hans was put in the next-to-lowest class. The boys were all much smaller and younger than he. And they all knew a lot more about history and geography and Latin than Hans did.

The teacher, Master Meisling, did not try to help Hans. He was a cruel man

who liked to make fun of boys —
especially boys who were different. Hans
was different from any boy Master
Meisling had ever seen before. He found
many ways to make fun of Hans.

Whenever Hans made a mistake in
class, Master Meisling shouted at him.
"Stupid!" he yelled. "I have never had
such a stupid boy in my class."

Hans shook with fear.

Sometimes Master Meisling made
jokes about the tall, homely Hans in
front of the whole class. All the little
boys would laugh at his cruel jokes, and
Hans would burst into tears.

"See the baby," Master Meisling would
say then. "Have you ever seen such a
big, ugly baby?" The hoots of laughter
made Hans cry even more.

Hans did not understand the teacher.
"Why is Master Meisling so angry with
me all the time?" he wondered. "Maybe
I am a dunce. What would Mr. Collin

think if he knew how stupid I really am? I must try to learn."

Hans did try. He studied hard. After a while, he could give the right answers to most of the questions Master Meisling asked him. He hoped that the teacher would stop making fun of him now. He wanted Master Meisling to like him.

And sometimes Master Meisling did seem to like Hans. He would be very friendly. But just when everything was going well, Master Meisling would make a cruel joke about Hans's looks. He would yell at Hans for no reason at all. Hans never knew what his teacher was going to do.

As the years went by, Hans learned how to get along with Master Meisling. But he never got used to feeling hurt and ashamed when Master Meisling made fun of him.

Hans went to school at Slagelse for four years. He grew from a boy of seventeen to a young man of twenty-one. During the years, he made many friends among boys his own age. He studied history and geography and Latin. He studied mathematics and French and his own language, Danish.

Hans wrote whenever he had time — mostly poems. Master Meisling told him to study, not waste time writing poems. But Hans thought his poems were as important as his studies, and he kept on writing them.

While he was going to school, Hans did not need all the money he got from Mr. Collin. He saved the extra money and sent it to his mother in Odense. She needed money. Her husband had died, and she was too old and sick to wash clothes in the river any more.

Then Hans had bad news. The few rix-dollars he gave his mother were not enough. She had been sent to live in the poorhouse.

The thought of his mother in the Odense poorhouse made Hans sad. He could hardly wait to finish school and start earning money. It would take a lot of money to get her out of the poorhouse.

In 1826, when Hans was twenty-one years old, Master Meisling took a job at another school. He asked Hans to go with him.

"If you come along, I will give you extra lessons," he said. "You will finish school in six months. If you stay here, you will not finish for a long time. What do you say?"

Hans knew right away what he was going to do. "I will go with you," he said to Master Meisling.

At the new school, things got worse for Hans. He had to live in the same house with Master Meisling and his family. The house was always dirty. Master Meisling and his wife and children were always dirty too.

The teacher still made jokes about Hans and called him names. He made fun of the poems Hans wrote. This hurt Hans more than anything else.

Hans had never been so unhappy in his life. At last he wrote to Mr. Collin: "I want to leave school. I am stupid and will never be a good writer. I will try to learn a trade instead. I am sorry I could not do better."

Mr. Collin could not believe what he read. Hans Christian Andersen wanted to learn a trade! No. Something must be wrong.

A few days later Mr. Collin found out what was wrong. Another teacher in the school wrote to him and told him about Master Meisling and Hans. No wonder Hans wanted to leave school! Mr. Collin thought. He wrote a letter to Hans. "Pack your clothes and come home," he said.

## The Writer, H. C. Andersen

MASTER MEISLING had made Hans feel stupid. But Hans had really learned a great deal in school. When he came back to Copenhagen, Mr. Collin sent him to a private teacher to finish his studies. Then, in October of 1828, Hans Christian Andersen took the examination at the University of Copenhagen. He passed. His days of studying were over.

Hans was twenty-three years old. He knew what he wanted to be — he wanted to be a famous writer. And now he could spend all his time writing. He already had an idea for a book.

Hans had always liked to walk in the city. He liked to walk along the docks and through the busy, narrow streets. Hans wrote a book about his favorite walk. He wrote about the people he saw and about the things he thought or dreamed of as he was walking along.

Many people in Copenhagen read the book written by H. C. Andersen. "This young man is a good writer," they said, and Hans was pleased.

Hans wrote poems too. Some were printed in newspapers and magazines. Then a book of his poems was printed.

Hans did not earn much money from his writing. He wished he would get rich. Then he could give his mother enough money so that she would not have to go on living in the poorhouse.

Four years passed, and the writer H. C. Andersen did not get rich. Sometimes he made some money when a poem of his was printed in a newspaper. He also made a little money by translating French plays into Danish. And he wrote the stories for two operas.

When he had saved a little money, Hans took a trip. He visited many places on the island of Jutland in Denmark. The next year he saved a little more money and took a trip to Germany.

Hans liked to travel. He met many kinds of people and saw many wonderful things. The people he met and the things he saw gave him ideas for poems and stories to write.

In 1832, Hans took another trip. He went to Odense, the town where he had been born.

Hans stopped to see Colonel Guldberg and his other old friends. Then he went to the poorhouse to see his mother.

When Mrs. Andersen saw her tall, grown-up son, she ran to him and put her arms around him. Her eyes were full of tears. Hans was crying too. He was sad to see how old and sick his mother was. He wanted to say something to make her happy.

"The people in Copenhagen read my poems and stories," he told her. "I will write more. Soon everyone in Denmark will know who I am. Soon I will be famous."

"That is what the wise woman said," his mother answered. "Remember? Long ago, she said you would become famous."

When it was time for Hans to go, he was sorry to leave his mother. He told her, "I will work hard. When I am rich, I will buy you a little house in the country. You will have a maid and a butler to wait on you."

Hans's mother never got the house in the country. A few months after Hans's visit, she died. Hans had not earned enough money to get her out of the poorhouse.

In 1833, Hans asked the King of Denmark for money to make a long trip. He wanted to see more of the world.

The King and the Danish government often helped writers and artists who did not have enough money to travel. They voted to let Hans have the money he needed.

Hans went to four countries — Germany, France, Switzerland, and Italy. He visited many cities and towns. He talked with many people — with other writers, with artists, with plain men, women, and children. He wrote in his diary about everything that happened on his trip. Sometimes he drew pictures of the places he saw.

When Hans came back to Copenhagen, he wrote a story called *Life in Italy*. It was sold all over the world — in Italy, Germany, France, and England, as well as in Denmark. Hans was making money at last. At last he was becoming famous.

The next book Hans wrote was called *Fairy Tales Told for Children*. Two of the tales were "The Princess and the Pea" and "The Tinder Box."

Hans had always liked to tell stories to children — now that he was a writer,

he would write them. Hans tried to write the stories the way he told them. He wanted his readers to be able to see everything as if they were watching a play.

Some of Hans's friends thought his fairy tales were better than anything else he had written. One friend said, "Your book *Life in Italy* will make you famous, Hans — but your fairy tales will make people remember you forever."

Hans didn't think his fairy tales were as good as his other books, but he liked to write them. Two years later he wrote "The Emperor's New Clothes" and "The Little Mermaid."

After a while, a new book of fairy tales by H. C. Andersen was printed every year around Christmas time — Hans's Christmas gift to children and grownups everywhere.

## "*My life is a beautiful fairy tale*"

A TALL MAN dressed in a beautiful black cape was walking along a street in Copenhagen. He wore a shiny silk top hat and white gloves. He was thin, and his face was not handsome. But it was a kind face that made people like him the moment they saw him.

Everyone on the street turned to stare at the man as he walked by.

"Who is that fine gentleman?" someone asked.

"That is Hans Christian Andersen, who writes the fairy tales."

Hans was an old man now. Thirty

years had gone by since he had written his first fairy tales. Now he had written more than one hundred fairy tales. And he wrote many other books. He wrote poems and plays and songs too. All the people of Denmark sang his songs. His books and poems were read by people all over the world. His plays were put on in the Royal Theater of Copenhagen. Hans had become a hero of the Danish people.

But it was the fairy tales that people had come to love most of all. Children and grownups loved the stories about the Ugly Duckling, the Steadfast Tin Soldier, Thumbelina, and all the others. Kings and princes loved Hans's fairy tales too. They invited Hans to their castles to read his stories to them. Hans

became a friend of the kings and queens, princes and princesses of many countries. He had friends everywhere — some were great writers and artists and scientists.

Hans was happy to have so many friends. He was happy that so many people liked to read his fairy tales. He was happy that he had become a famous man. But sometimes Hans felt lonely. He was never married. He never had children of his own. And yet there were thousands of children who loved him — children all over the world who listened to his fairy tales.

When Hans was sixty-two years old, he was invited to a celebration. It was to be held in the town of Odense. The people of the town were proud of Hans. They wanted to thank him for all the wonderful stories he had given the world. And so they were having a celebration in honor of Hans Christian Andersen, who had been born in their city.

On December 4, 1867, Hans took the train from Copenhagen to Odense. As he rode in the train he thought of all the trips he had made by stagecoach before trains were invented. Mostly he thought about the trip he had made from Odense to Copenhagen forty-eight years ago, when he was fourteen.

The celebration for Hans Christian Andersen lasted a week. The people of Odense cheered him and waved flags when he rode down the street. The mayor and other important people in the town gave speeches about the famous writer. The schools were closed so that the children could join the celebration. They sang a song for Andersen and gave him flowers.

One day all the children of Odense

came to the city hall so that Hans Christian Andersen could read one of his stories to them.

One night there was a parade for Andersen. People marched in the street, singing a song he had written. They carried lighted torches.

When Hans came out on a balcony to see the parade, the people cried, "Hurrah! Hurrah! Long live Hans Christian Andersen!"

Hans's heart was filled with joy. He looked out at the people. Then he looked out past the bright torches — out into the dark, toward the house where he had been born.

He thought about his mother and father and about himself when he was a poor child. He thought about all the things that had happened to him since he left Odense.

Then he remembered the words of the wise woman who had told his mother, "Your son will become a great man. . . . One day the town of Odense will pay him a great honor. Everyone will hold a lighted torch to salute him." It had all come true.

Hans said a silent prayer. He thanked God for giving him such a wonderful life. "My life is a beautiful fairy tale," he thought. And so it was.